# 58 Ways to Leverage the Public Domain for Profit

A Guide to Using the Public Domain to Grow Your Business

by

Steven Chabotte

Copyright © 2010

Steven Chabotte & THA New Media Corp

All rights reserved.

This publication is for your personal use only. It comes with no other rights.

No part of this publication may be reproduced or transmitted in any form by any means, mechanical or electronic, including photocopying and recording, or by any information storage and retrieval system, without permission in writing from the publisher.

Legal Notices

While all attempts have been made to verify the information provided in this publication, neither the author or publisher assumes any responsibility for any errors, omissions or contrary interpretation of the subject matter herein.

This publication and all supporting materials is an information product. It does not offer legal, accounting or tax advice. The reader assumes all responsibility for the use of all materials and information presented herein, including adherence to all applicable laws and regulations.

This material is presented for educational purposes only. It offers no guarantees of any specific level of income, sales or results that can be achieved as a result of applying the information contained herein. Any figures offered are for illustration purposes only and/or derived from actual results of the author. They do not represent any specific results that the reader will achieve by applying the materials contained herein.

The purchaser or reader of this publication assumes all responsibility for the use of these materials and information. Adherence to all applicable laws and regulations is the sole responsibility of the purchaser or reader. The author and publisher assume no responsibility or liability whatsoever on the behalf of any purchaser or reader of these materials.

Any perceived slights of specific people or organizations in unintentional.

# CONTENTS

|     | INTRODUCTION | 1 |
| --- | --- | --- |
| 1   | PUBLISH THE WORK AS IS | 2 |
| 2   | CONVERT WORK TO AN AUTORESPONDER | 4 |
| 3   | CREATE FREE REPORTS | 6 |
| 4   | REPURPOSE CONTENT | 8 |
| 5   | PUBLIC DOMAIN IMAGES | 9 |
| 6   | CONVERT A BOOK TO AUDIO | 11 |
| 7   | CREATE A SERIES OF LESSONS | 13 |
| 8   | BUILD A SERIES OF YOUTUBE VIDEOS | 15 |
| 9   | REWRITE CONTENT TO CREATE ARTICLES | 17 |
| 10  | USE PUBLIC DOMAIN IMAGE/FILM CLIPS IN YOUR VIDEO PRODUCTIONS | 18 |
| 11  | MAKE A DOCUMENTARY | 19 |
| 12  | CONVERT A BOOK INTO A TRAINING PACKAGE | 20 |
| 13  | REWRITE CONTENT TO CREATE ARTICLES | 22 |
| 14  | BUILD WORKSHEETS AND CHECKLISTS | 23 |
| 15  | CREATE ADD ON PRODUCTS | 25 |
| 16  | BUILD A RETRO/NOSTALGIA WEBSITE | 26 |
| 17  | OPEN SOURCE SOFTWARE TRAINING GUIDES | 28 |
| 18  | BUILD ADDONS TO OPEN SOURCE SOFTWARE | 29 |
| 19  | BRAND OPEN SOURCE SOFTWARE | 30 |
| 20  | REWRITE CONTENT TO CREATE ARTICLES | 31 |
| 21  | CREATE A VIRAL PRODUCT | 32 |
| 22  | PUBLIC DOMAIN MASHUP | 33 |
| 23  | ADVERTISER SUPPORTED WEBSITE | 34 |

| 24 | NEWSLETTER ISSUES | 35 |
| 25 | BUILD A MEMBERSHIP SITE | 36 |
| 26 | PODCASTS | 37 |
| 27 | ARTICLE SPINNER SOURCE MATERIAL | 38 |
| 28 | PLR CONTENT | 39 |
| 29 | POSTERS/ARTWORK | 40 |
| 30 | RESALE/MASTER RESALE RIGHTS | 41 |
| 31 | BUILD TRAINING GUIDES | 42 |
| 32 | CREATE A COFFEE TABLE BOOK | 43 |
| 33 | REPUBLISH OLD COMICS | 44 |
| 34 | CREATE A MOVIE SCRIPT | 45 |
| 35 | CREATE A SEMINAR | 46 |
| 36 | BUILD TRUST | 47 |
| 37 | FREEBIES FOR LIVE EVENTS | 48 |
| 38 | CONVERT FOR NEW MEDIA DEVICES | 49 |
| 39 | BUILD A WIKI SITE | 50 |
| 40 | PHYSICAL PRODUCTS | 51 |
| 41 | PUBLIC DOMAIN NEWSPAPERS | 52 |
| 42 | BUILD A DIRECTORY | 53 |
| 43 | LOCAL AD BOOK | 54 |
| 44 | HOMESCHOOLING MATERIALS | 55 |
| 45 | CORPORATE TRAINING | 56 |
| 46 | PATENTS | 57 |
| 47 | CALENDARS | 58 |
| 48 | NOSTALGIA PRODUCTS | 59 |
| 49 | DATABASES | 60 |

| 50 | GENEALOGY | 61 |
| 51 | HISTORIC MAPS | 62 |
| 52 | AFFILIATE LINKS | 63 |
| 53 | SEED A FORUM | 64 |
| 54 | TRANSLATION | 65 |
| 55 | CONTENT FOR REPLIES | 66 |
| 56 | INTERACTIVE WEBSITES | 67 |
| 57 | BONUS PRODUCTS | 68 |
| 58 | ENHANCE YOUR LIFE | 69 |
|    | END NOTE | 70 |

# INTRODUCTION

The public domain is a very powerful resource for your business. There is content out there – both in old materials that are no longer under copyright protection and new materials produced by the U.S. Government or donated to the public domain – that can help you in any type of business.

The true power of public domain materials is that they come with absolutely no strings attached. You can literally do anything you want with them.

It is our hope that this report gives you a few ideas on how you can use public domain materials profitably in your business.

Best Wishes,

Steven

# 1 PUBLISH THE WORK AS IS

Taking a public domain work and republishing it is the first and easiest method of using materials in the public domain.

There are many ways that a public domain work can be republished.

It can be republished as:

1. A physical book – either a short run at a vanity publisher or by utilizing a publish on demand company like Cafepress, Lulu or Createspace.

2. An ebook.

3. A website or section of a website that has its pages, the pages of the book.

4. A copy of the book on CD or DVD.

5. In the case of a public domain movie, it can be digitized and burned to a DVD or made into a movie viewable on the web.

6. In the case of audio, it could be made into a CD or web based delivery via MP3s.


I'm sure you can think of a few additional ways you can take a book, report, audio recording, film or other type of public domain work and package it in a format that can be delivered to customers.

In this particular model, the work effort is in formatting the work to fit into the type of media you will be using. No effort is made in actually changing the work in any way. Thus a book put on a CD is identical to the original published book except it is now a digital copy.

How you choose to republish the work will depend on what you plan on doing with it once it is republished. Some ideas include:

Giving away an electronic copy on your website

Giving away printed copies at a seminar

Selling copies to your customers

Using copies as a bonus to another item you are selling

## 2 CONVERT WORK TO AN AUTORESPONDER

The great thing about public domain materials is that you can use them in any way you see fit. And one very powerful technique is to use the materials as an autoresponder sequence – either as is or massaged to fit the message you are delivering.

A great example of an autoresponder series offering as is content could be something like "Marketing Secrets of the Ancient Masters." In this example, you could take extracts from several of the masters of marketing who were publishing in the early 1900s. Each chapter could be a specific lesson from a master.

An example of offering massaged content can be a simple spin on the above idea: "Marketing Secrets of the Ancient Masters – Updated for the Internet." In this example, you would take the essence of each lesson and rework it to reflect modern web based ways to utilize it in a business. Or maybe you just deliver the entire original lesson followed by several paragraphs showing how it can be updated and used today.

Autoresponder series like this can be used in your business in several ways. Some examples include:

They can be used as a way to collect email addresses as people sign up for your series.

They can be used as lead ins to market your own products that are related to the subject being discussed in each autoresponder email.

They can be embedded with links that will generate affiliate commissions.

You could even let people purchase the entire collection as a complete book or ebook.

The autoresponder service we use and recommend is Aweber. They have been around since 1998 and offer reliable and quality service.

# 3 CREATE FREE REPORTS

One of the most powerful ways to market is to give away something for free. And public domain content is a great way to create high quality free reports with a minimal time investment. In some cases, the reports can be direct copies of public domain works. In others, some massaging might be needed.

If you are working on a project that requires timely information, finding U.S. Government reports on the topic might offer perfect as is works for your free reports. If the subject is less timely, or a timeless subject, you will be able to find any number of public domain works related to it that can be used as is or with just a little massaging.

Just to get an idea of what some timely reports might look like, take a look at what is offered at the Federal Citizens Information Center. There are literally hundreds of reports there that could be used as is on a variety of subjects – computers, business, finance, health, etc. And since they are public domain works, you can just copy the content and reformat it with your own branding elements and have a great free report to offer.

There are many ways you can use free reports. You can use them as:

Giveaways to people who subscribe to your mailing list.

Product bonuses to help increase sales

Content for websites, blogs, etc.

Interesting follow-up emails in autoresponder sequences

Handouts at seminars

As leave behind materials with potential clients

and many other ways...

# 4 REPURPOSE CONTENT

While there are many occasions where you can use public domain content as is, repurposing it is many times more powerful for your business.

So what does repurposing mean?

Put simply, it means using and recombining public domain works in different ways. This can include extracting sections from multiple works to create a new work, rewriting an existing work to expand it or make it more up to date or converting it from one form to another. For instance, you could create an audiobook or convert a book into a series of lessons.

There really is no limit to how you can repurpose public domain content. Your imagination is the limit.

If you question how powerful it is, just go to Google and do a search on Bible lessons. There are many successful companies making good money teaching the lessons of the Bible.

# 5 PUBLIC DOMAIN IMAGES

One of the great things about the public domain is the fascinating images that are available.

Just think about it... Every book, magazine, newspaper, postcard, poster, movie, architectural drawing, patent and other work in the public domain that has images in it means that it has images you can potentially use.

That is what is so great about public domain works. You do not need to keep them intact. You can extract what you need. That means you can take an image from one book, three from another book, etc. and build a product from it.

As an example, Dover Press has a large number of themed clip art collections, all built using images from public domain works. In fact, many of the books they sell are public domain works and these works allowed them to build a large company.

Here are a few ways you can use public domain images to get your imagination flowing.

You can use them as graphics when designing your website.

Are you creating an ebook cover? There is probably a perfect public domain image available for your use.

Are you a blogger? Why not liven up your posts with images.

How about building your own themed clip art library to offer for sale. All it takes is a little investigation and a bunch of editing to pull it all together. And it could give you a product that you could sell for years.

How about artwork on a t shirt or a coffee mug

If your business is creating artwork, what would an unlimited supply of high quality artwork do to help you meet clients needs?

How about making a narrated slide show? You could put it on YouTube and possible have it go viral on you.

There are many, many more possibilities. What others can you come up with?

# 6 CONVERT A BOOK TO AUDIO

Changing the form of a book from the written word to audio can create a whole new market for the item. If you've looked at products for any length of time, you have seen many examples of physical books turned into audio books and sold that way. Just go to your local bookstore and you will see many examples of this.

So how can this work for public domain works?

One powerful method a few enterprising entrepreneurs are using is giving away the book as a free pdf download and offering the audio book version for sale. This gives them the viral power of a free giveaway with a valuable back end which didn't take a great deal of effort to create.

Another spin some folks do is to convert the written book into an audio lesson plan. This takes a bit more work as you are distilling the teachings in the book into new audio content. What these authors are doing is using the audio to extend the lessons taught in the book. This method allows you to create a higher value product than a direct audio book would have.

What is great about working with the audio is that it gives you a variety of promotional activities to get the word out about your product.

In addition to giving away a pdf copy of the book, you can also give away an audio chapter or audio lesson as a podcast or a free download on your website or blog. This is a great way to let folks experience what they are getting before committing to a purchase.

And of course you can always give away the entire audio series that you created if you tied it into some promotion for what you are selling. For instance, if the book had ten chapters, you would create an audio for each chapter and at the beginning and/or end of the audio chapter, you would place an audio commercial for what you are selling.

This method is quite powerful for generating more business.

# 7 CREATE A SERIES OF LESSONS

Creating a series of lessons – or a training course – out of a public domain work or series of related works is my favorite method of creating high dollar value products. And sometimes – of the original source material is well known – you get a huge publicity boost from the associated name recognition.

There are many different ways you can create lessons out of a work. And the lessons can be presented in multiple formats.

In looking at the formats...

You could build written lessons with a workbook of exercises to guide the student's learning.

You could build a series of audio lessons.

You could build a series of powerpoint presentations.

You could create a mixed media product that incorporated written materials, video and audio materials.

The lesson plans themselves can be created in a variety of styles. (In fact, you could create a whole series of lesson plans based on a book.)

For instance, you could

be quite literal in your lessons and take exactly what is written in the book but now offer it in lesson format. Each lesson would exactly teach what was in each chapter with exercises, etc. to help understand the material.

expand on what is taught in each chapter of a book, building a series of lessons to fill in the holes.

create a whole new lesson series loosely based on the teachings of the book but totally presented from your own unique perspective.

combine materials from multiple books to produce a totally unique set of lessons on a topic. (If you are not getting name recognition from the original source material, this method is quite powerful because it doesn't limit you to any particular framework. You can pull out the best bits from multiple sources and build a new, more powerful product than any of the original products.)

# 8 BUILD A SERIES OF YOUTUBE VIDEOS

Video is all the rage nowadays and what better way to use public domain material than to make your own videos to post to youtube (or for other uses.)

With just a few tools and some public domain works you can on your way to video stardom. Tools like Sony Movie Studio, Camtasia, or Microsoft Movie Maker are all you need to produce some really high quality video productions. Productions can either be movies, slide shows, powerpoint type presentations, visual teaching guides or some combination of the above.

With public domain materials,

you can find all the stock footage you can ever need to create your works. A massive collection of stock footage can be found at http://www.archive.org/details/stock_footage. And while you are there, be sure to check out all the other film sections. You can cut pieces out of them to build your own stock footage – but be sure they are in the public domain first. (Oh, and they have a great public domain audio section that you can use for background music in your productions.

 Stock images can be pulled from any public domain book, magazine, poster, postcard, etc. All you need is the source material and a scanner (or graphics program to cut the image if the source material is already in digital format.)

you can use book chapters and content to build your presentation. This essential research can be used to build a script for a training video on a particular subject.

Before making a youtube video on a particular subject, it is always good to take a few moments to look at what videos are already posted on that subject. Study them and take notes about what was powerful and what turned you off. Use that knowledge when you script out your own videos.

The key to success with youtube videos is to keep them short and keep them targeted. If you can teach something clearly and completely in three minutes, that is how long the video should be. If it takes five minutes, it should be a five minute video. If you are teaching a complex subject, break it up into small digestible parts and build a series of videos to teach the whole thing.

And remember, the ultimate purpose of making the youtube videos is to benefit your business. So be sure to give people a reason to contact you or visit your website in every video you publish.

# 9 REWRITE CONTENT TO CREATE ARTICLES

Everyone knows that articles are powerful. So why not use a public domain book as the platform to launch a series of articles on a particular topic. How many articles do you think you can get from a 300 page book (or several books) on your topic? Especially when you have totally free use of the content?

Once you create your article/article series, you can use the material in many ways:

submissions to article directories

content for your blog

get it published in a trade journal

post it on your website

use it as an autoresponder series

release it as a series of white papers

Use them in your newsletter

I'm sure you can come up with many other ways to use articles but this list should be enough to get the creative juices flowing.

# 10 USE PUBLIC DOMAIN IMAGE/FILM CLIPS IN YOUR VIDEO PRODUCTIONS

A quality video production can be a very valuable asset to your company.

The challenge often faced in video product is in finding just the right clip to convey the message. Even if you are doing a talking head video, you might want to break it up with relevant images from time to time.

Before so much digitized public domain material was readily accessible on the internet, finding the correct image or video clip often meant going to a company that made available royalty free images and videos. While they have extensive libraries, their prices were most often too prohibitive for the small video producer, relegating them to second class citizens in the video quality department.

That is no longer the case as there is an endless variety of already predigitized public domain material covering just about any subject available for free download on the web. It might take a bit of searching to find exactly what you are looking for but chances are that perfect bit that will make your video production shine is sitting out there waiting for you to discover it.

# 11 MAKE A DOCUMENTARY

Well done documentaries on a subject can be very powerful – and can make you a good deal of money.

Now before you get the wrong idea, documentaries don't have to be about World War II or any historical events, they have be absolutely current. By utilizing government videos, graphs and statistics, you can build a documentary about almost any current subject.

If you ran a marketing company, build a documentary on the seismic change to marketing since the dawn of the internet. If you are into alternative energy, build one on the march of progress of alternative energy solutions. (And of course, if it tickles your fancy, make a historical documentary. There is always a market for a new angle on a historical event.

Even if you cannot make a direct profit from a documentary, its a great marketing tool. Imagine telling a prospect to see your documentary on youtube. Do you think it will help you generate business?

# 12 CONVERT A BOOK INTO A TRAINING PACKAGE

A training program is a perceived high value item but it can take quite a bit of work to build one from scratch. Why not use a public domain book or series of books on the topic as the basis for your training package.

Your training package can be a series of written lessons, audio lessons, video lessons, flowcharts and diagrams, checklists, exercises, etc.

Creating a training package is pretty simple. If you are using a single book as the basis, read through the book and figure out how to convert its knowledge into logical modules, each one building on the other one.

For instance, you would start with an overview module that tells what the course is all about, how it is organized, if it should be worked in any particular order and a brief statement about what each of the additional modules contain. The rest of the modules are all focused on a single idea per module and concentrate the effort on really nailing down what that idea is about.

Once you create your list of modules, you will then make an outline of what each module will contain and how it will be structured – i.e. just text, or is there a video component or worksheets to go along with the module, etc.

Once you know what is going to be contained in each modules, it is simply a matter of filling in the details, producing any videos, audios, worksheets, etc. for it and repeating it for each of the modules until the entire training program is completed.

A training program can seem intimidating as there are potentially many parts to it but if you work it one section at a time (or one media element at a time), it will get built quicker than you can ever imagine.

Oh, if you have an opportunity, you should pick up some training programs to study how they are put together and do so with a critical eye. It is a great way to discern the strengths and weaknesses of others materials so you can build a really strong program.

# 13 REWRITE CONTENT TO CREATE ARTICLES

We all face information overload so any way to learn something faster and more clearly has value to us. Mind maps are a powerful technique used to capture materials in a one page diagram.

If you take a public domain book or other matter and create a mind map out of it, it will have value to others. This means you can use this mind map as a giveaway to grow a list, use it as a bonus for another product, bundle it in with a digital copy of the public domain work and sell it as a package (i.e. creating a value added scenario to the original work), use it as the basis of a presentation, etc.

Don't shortchange the idea of a mind map as a product. Even though it is only one page, it will be quite valuable to people interested in that subject area.

# 14 BUILD WORKSHEETS AND CHECKLISTS

Worksheets and checklists are great tools because they allow us to absorb materials and take action very quickly. That take material that is passive and makes it active.

Why is this important?

It is important because we absorb the most material when we are active participants. Think about it. If you read a book, it is soon forgotten. If you read the same book with a highlighter and a notebook at hand (and use them), the material stays with you much longer.

Worksheets act as that highlighter and note book on steroids because they are telling you what you should be getting from a particular section of material. They then guide your understanding of the material with a series of short exercises to help reinforce what you are learning and really to force you to reflect on and interpret what you are learning.

Checklists are powerful after the fact materials. Once you learned something, they help you take action by outlining the specific steps you need to take to perform a particular task in the specific order they need to be performed in for success.

Worksheets and checklists are a tremendous value add to any discipline and make solid standalone products.

Here is an example that most marketers can relate to.

Wordpress, an open source software package, is a very powerful software package. And with all the enhancements (plugins) available, it can be very complex to set up optimally for an SEO optimized blog. A series of checklists of all the tasks that are needed to accomplish this is quite valuable. In this example, the checklists would include what plugins to use, the optimal settings of each one, how to lay out your blog once all the plugins are installed and finally how to optimally post each message for maximum results. Now wouldn't that be useful?

# 15 CREATE ADD ON PRODUCTS

Many people create success by piggybacking on success.

If a public domain work is still popular today, many add on products can be created and sold.

Consider the very famous book "The Art of War." Right now on Amazon, there are over two thousand variations and spinoffs of this one book being sold.

Or consider the Bible. There are so many variations and spinoffs created from the teachings of the Bible that it is impossible to count them.

So next time you are stuck for ideas, consider an add on product.

# 16 BUILD A RETRO/NOSTALGIA WEBSITE

Everyone know fan websites are popular. After all, celebrities are always in the news and fans have an insatiable appetite for any and all things related to their celebrity.

That same insatiable appetite exists in the nostalgia and retro markets – and the best part is they can all be built with public domain materials so there are never any worries about ownership issues over images and other content.

So what might be a retro or nostalgia website?

It can be just about anything that has fans. Consider the 1957 Chevy – a car with a cult following. A car that when an exact match on google of "57 Chevy" is performed, almost one million pages are returned. Do you think there are folks interested in 57 Chevy's?

So why not take that type of market and build a fan site for it. You can fill it in with information about the cars, the accessories, photos, period ads, etc. and members can add their own photos and share their ownership experiences. You could even put in a swap section so folks can buy and sell 57 Chevy items to each other.

If cars are not your thing, how about old motorcycles, boats, vending machines? And if you really are hooked on doing a fan club, how about "Heartthrobs of the 1950's" or something similar. You can find tons of neat information about them in period magazines, many of which will be in the public domain.

The nostalgia market is huge. You just need to choose your niche, dominate it and monetize it – all based on free public domain content.

# 17 OPEN SOURCE SOFTWARE TRAINING GUIDES

Lets face it. Software is hard to use. And the documentation provided is quite often very poor. That is why there is such a thriving business selling training books, video tutorials, camtasia tutorials, etc. for popular software packages.

The value of these materials is related to the value that can be delivered by using the software well. This is why the most valuable training guides are for software programming tools, business productivity tools and of course game cheat guides.

This demand exists whether the software was purchased or a free open source download. If the tool can help someone do X better, that person will pay to learn how to use it more effectively.

So maybe it is time to polish off your research and writing skills and create the ultimate Wordpress or Joomla training guide (just two of the hundreds of really popular open source software products out there.)

# 18 BUILD ADDONS TO OPEN SOURCE SOFTWARE

One of the great things about open source software is that people can expand its functionality by creating addons or plugins.

Some popular open source software packages – wordpress for instance – literally have thousands of addons available to them. (In the case of wordpress, there are tons of free plugins and themes and a few paid ones that are quite popular.)

So if you have programming skills – or a great idea and can hire a programmer – you can make a good income with your own open source addon.

Three of the many ways people use their addons include:

Selling it

Giving it away for free and asking for donations to support future development

Giving it away for free to help build a mailing list.

## 19 BRAND OPEN SOURCE SOFTWARE

There are many powerful free applications available with open source licenses. You can do whatever you want with them as long as you adhere to the open source license. This includes making modifications to the source code and distributing your version under the terms of the license agreement.

One great way to use this in your business is to find an application that would fit your marketplace, brand it and offer it as a giveaway to anyone who wants to download it. Since most folks do not know about open source code, they will really appreciate you making this killer application available to them in exchange for signing up for your mailing list.

There are many twists to this basic concept that you can use with a little thought and imagination.

# 20 REWRITE CONTENT TO CREATE ARTICLES

Teleseminars and webinars are big business. And one way to quickly create a dynamic presentation is to find public domain sources to help you.

Public domain works can either provide the entire outline of the course you wish to teach via this media option or bits and pieces – such as supporting graphics, images, charts, etc. that help build more credibility into your presentation.

## 21 CREATE A VIRAL PRODUCT

Nothing helps you build traffic to your business better than a product that goes viral. Why not use some public domain works to help you craft some pieces with viral potential.

As one example, you could create a motivational tip/image of the day application that either emails out the motivational message every day or displays it on a website with some promotional materials and has a hook to some form of "Tell a Friend" script.

Or a tip of the day/week type newsletter related to your business niche. It can all be programmed up into aweber and run on autopilot. Combine it with a "Tell a Friend" script to ramp up the viral factor. And the best part is tips are expected to be short – just a few paragraphs so in a few hours you can literally create a year's worth of follow up emails – especially if you have a public domain work to pull from.

## 22 PUBLIC DOMAIN MASHUP

In this idea, you create a brand new work by combining bits and pieces of several public domain works.

Some of the many examples of this idea include famous quotations, niche recipes, tip books, clip art collections.

# 23 ADVERTISER SUPPORTED WEBSITE

Building quality websites is important for all your web activities and public domain works give you a way to quickly build quality themed websites. These websites can be used by you to sell advertising space, use for affiliate sales, adsense, etc. (And they can be used to help you build a mailing list.)

There are many ways you can approach this.

For instance, you could take a related collection of books and break them up into their chapters. They post each chapter on a blog and encourage people to comment on each chapter to make it interactive.

Or you can just make each page in the book a page on the website and allow people to read it by clicking from page to page (with each page having advertising on it.)

As a value add, you could find relevant images and "illustrate" your web version of the book to make it more visually appealing.

## 24 NEWSLETTER ISSUES

Writing a quality newsletter – whether it be physically printed or emailed – can be a time consuming process when done from scratch.

With public domain materials, you can dramatically shorten this process. You can use the materials as excerpts to support your argument, use as is or update to make relevant to your audience, get great clipart to spice up your newsletter or as a source of ideas to include in various issues.

As long as the material is interesting and relevant to your audience, they will not care if it is brand new material. The key is relevance. We are all happy reading something that helps us in our endeavor and none of us care if it was written 100 years ago or just yesterday as long as it moves us forward.

## 25 BUILD A MEMBERSHIP SITE

Public domain material – especially government materials – can make the basis of a very profitable membership site. When thinking about this idea, you have to remember that people are paying you for bringing together material that is valuable to them in one place.

So your membership site might be all the new regulations constantly being issued by the government on some issue or all the latest research reports on a particular topic.

And of course some folks have created membership sites by packing themed public domain works with sales materials that the members can use in any way they want – sort of a monthly business in a box idea.

# 26 PODCASTS

If you create a podcast on a popular topic and upload it to a podcast distribution site, you have an opportunity to get your podcast listened to by thousands.

Using public domain works as is or as the basis for the podcast is a great way to shorten the development time of your podcast script. Time time leverage factor will let you get several podcasts done in the time it would take to create one from scratch.

## 27 ARTICLE SPINNER SOURCE MATERIAL

Since you can do whatever you want with public domain works, why not use it as the root piece of material to plug into article spinner software to generate dozens of variations that you can post all over the web to help promote your website.

One good product to help you professionally spin your articles is Rapid Rewriter. Not only is it an excellent software package, it also comes with complete training on how to use your newly spun article collection for maximum impact.

# 28 PLR CONTENT

There are many folks willing to pay good money for high quality PLR content in niche markets. With public domain works, you could literally create 1000's of new, quality PLR works in any niche you choose.

So if you are a person who enjoys digging through the materials, extracting important points from the material and cleaning it up so it flows nice, you can build yourself a good income. A single 200 page book on a subject can contribute heavily to dozens of PLR articles on that subject.

## 29 POSTERS/ARTWORK

If you are good with the turn of a phrase, creating posters that combine public domain images and a catchy phrase might be the business you are looking for. Ideas can include inspirational posters, humorous posters, posters designed to make you pause and think, etc.

Or if you are artistically minded, you could find a new career turning public domain images into new works of art. You could use a public domain image and turn it into a watercolor. Or take a black and white image and colorize it to make it new and unique.

With the relatively low cost of wide format printers, you could even become your own poster/print publish on demand operation. Or you could link your works to one of the many companies that will publish on demand for you and just concentrate on the creative and promotional aspects of this business.

## 30 RESALE/MASTER RESALE RIGHTS

If you have the ability to take public domain works and turn them into valuable products, you can also repackage these products and sell resale rights to these products.

Resale rights give others the right to distribute your works under the rights terms you offer. Master resale rights allows the buyer to also sell resale rights to the product to others.

Many marketers make a full time income offering resale rights of some sort or other to their product. So why not you? It is certainly something to think about as you are massaging a public domain work for sale.

# 31 BUILD TRAINING GUIDES

Public domain works can be the basis of great training guides for your business or industry.

For instance, if you are in the network marketing industry, do you think your downline would find a time management course, goal management course, or basic course on copyrighting useful?

Just find a public domain work on the subject in question and massage it into a training guide that speaks to your audience and you will have a powerful guide that will benefit all your readers.

And even though I used network marketing as an example, it could be in any industry, hobby, sport, etc. Just let your imagination and interests guide you.

## 32 CREATE A COFFEE TABLE BOOK

Since there is so much great pictorial content in the public domain, you have the opportunity to make great coffee table books on an almost unlimited number of subjects. Coffee table books are those books that are mostly intriguing images of a topic with a small caption for each image.

Just to name a few ideas, you could make one for the Civil War, Pulp Fiction covers, birds of the world, architectural wonders, patents that changed the world, etc. The list is practically endless.

## 33 REPUBLISH OLD COMICS

In case you haven't noticed, comic anthologies are big business. And there are tons of great old comics that are in the public domain.

It would be a fairly simple task to gather up several comics – either a series or an assortment related to a theme or a particular publisher – and add some commentary and come up with a unique and in demand product.

If you do a search for public domain comics, you will find a variety of sources of already digitized material.

## 34 CREATE A MOVIE SCRIPT

Many written works have been turned into movies – in some cases multiple times.

Writing a script starts with creating a movie treatment and marketing it to film studios. Once they accept the treatment, a script is developed.

So rather than trying to come up with an innovative idea from scratch, why not start with the classics and figure out how you can tell an old story with a new twist.

Just do a search on your favorite search engine for the phrase "movie treatment" to begin your education in this fascinating and potentially lucrative field.

## 35 CREATE A SEMINAR

Public domain content can be perfect for creating a seminar. If you find the right materials, all the prep work is already done for you.

Your job would be to master the material and figure out a sensible presentation order for the materials to give the attendees a good experience. The materials should help you create your PowerPoint slides and any handouts you want to offer.

Also, don't be afraid to use public domain materials as a starting point. Often taking an old work and updating it is all it takes to create a popular up to date seminar. Or find a new twist on an already known work to make a new and unique presentation – like Samurai marketing for dentists or something like that.

## 36 BUILD TRUST

One of the biggest challenges of online businesses is to build trust.

Lets face it... doing business online is very different than in a retail setting. You can offer guarantees, generous return privileges and other trust items in your advertising but nothing helps build trust more than offering free materials that benefit your customer (or being a published author which lends a great deal of trust as long as the work is related to what you are selling.)

The great part here is you can reposition public domain works with your name or company name so for instance you can take government reports on credit card fraud and how to prevent it, repackage it with your company name and give it to visitors as a free download. It will show them how serious you are about making sure they are protected from fraudulent transactions. Not a bad return for a few minutes of work.

## 37 FREEBIES FOR LIVE EVENTS

Everyone who attends live events likes to go home with something in their hand. And this is a perfect use for public domain works.

For very little money, you could take any public domain work and reprint it as a professional looking physical book using one of the many publish on demand companies.

And of course, you can rebrand the book to be from you, add literature to it promoting your company, etc.

And unlike handouts, books have a long shelf life (no pun intended.) People generally hold on to books for years and that means that your materials are going to be in their hands for a very long time, reminding them of you and your services.

## 38 CONVERT FOR NEW MEDIA DEVICES

People are crazy for all the new devices coming out – ebook readers, ipads, more and more capable phones, notebook computers, etc.

And they are hungry for content that works with their new devices. So why not provide it.

All you need to do is convert existing public domain content into a format compatible with these devices and you will have an audience hungry for materials for their new devices lining up to buy it.

# 39 BUILD A WIKI SITE

We all know Google loves authority sites so why not build your own wiki on a subject. Use public domain materials to get it initially populated and then let it do what wikis are best for – building collaborative content on a subject.

Just think – if you built one on advertising, there are tons of books and fascinating ads in the public domain that could be posted as seed content. And once the collaborative effort starts, the site can explode.

To monetize it, you can use it to build a mailing list, promote your own products or affiliate products. And since you own it, you could even sell it to another entity for a very nice payoff down the road.

# 40 PHYSICAL PRODUCTS

In this idea, you can take public domain works and create physical products from them. In this instance, I'm referring to t shirts, calendars, coffee mugs, etc. They take only minutes to create and there are many companies that will make the actual product for you on a publish on demand basis so you don't have to inventory products.

You could build a calendar with Civil War images and important dates from the Civil War, a coffee mug from an old adventure comic or a t shirt with an image and edgy expression on it.

There are literally thousands of ways to spin this idea into various physical product. All it takes is a little effort and a sense of what the market would love to be able to turn this into a good money maker for you.

And with publish on demand technology, you can even create a one of a kind item just for you.

# 41 PUBLIC DOMAIN NEWSPAPERS

There are literally tons of things you can do with public domain newspapers. You can use a collection of stories to create a book about an important event in history as seen through the eyes of reporters, create genealogy research products, build a collection of fascinating old ads, a recurring newsletter of sports history, etc.

One of the ideas I really like is using the material to build "On This Day In History" type of products. There is a huge nostalgia demand for products that target a person's birth date. They can can be as specific as the actual day of birth (for instance a collection of newspapers on CD for that day) or birth month or just the most interesting news of that birth year.

If you invest a little time brainstorming, I'm sure you can come up with many more ideas that this source of public domain material can be used for.

## 42 BUILD A DIRECTORY

One goal every smart website owner has is to build pages on their websites that are magnets for incoming links.

One of the most powerful types of pages to induce this situation are directories/resource lists. They are very simple to create.

All you need to do is create a page with links to say 20, 30, 40 or so public domain works related to the subject of your website or blog.

A page like this can be created relatively quickly. It would just be a bulleted or numbered list of resources with a one line description of each and a link to go to each resource.

Pages like this – when well done – can result in hundreds of incoming links to that page. And that means lots of traffic to that page. So when implementing this idea, give lots of thought to how you want to use the traffic coming to that page so you can incorporate it into the design.

# 43 LOCAL AD BOOK

One concept that is very powerful is combining public domain material relevant to a community with ads from local merchants. This project could be a short book about interesting historical events in the community, a picture book of historic houses or even a historic map of the area.

Once the content is chosen, you would print up a mockup of the product (perhaps using a publish on demand company) and go to local businesses to sell ad space in the item.

For distribution, you can either print a large number of them and give some to each of the merchants who advertised to give away to their customers, distribute them to local hotels as a giveaway or offer them for sale through several local outlets.

In the right community, there are people making very large incomes from this one idea.

# 44 HOMESCHOOLING MATERIALS

Homeschooling is a large and growing industry in this country. And parents are hungry for quality materials to help them teach their children important topics.

Generally, people who homeschool have to purchase a specific curriculum to meet state guidelines but they often choose to supplement this material with other learning aids – both to help the children learn and to make it easier for them as well.

That makes a big market for materials that can easily and clearly present subject matter to the student as well as offering an associated teacher's guide to help the parents work with their children to master the materials.

While not a trivial task, it is fairly easy to take a public domain work on a subject and convert it into a dynamic lesson plan that excites both the child and parents. And if you can come up with that winning combination, a huge market is waiting to buy your materials.

# 45 CORPORATE TRAINING

Corporate training materials can be large money makers. Trainings can sell for several hundred to several thousand dollars and even more if they are live trainings. Trainings can include topics like complying with government regulations, time management, quality trainings, sales trainings, etc.

The key and challenge in getting into the corporate training market is to be perceived as an expert in that field. If managers think you are an expert, you have a good chance to sell your materials as you are a known quantity, not some stranger off the street.

Bob Bly has an excellent audio course on how to Become an Instant Guru. If you want success in this marketplace, this course will give you the foundation to open many doors for you.

# 46 PATENTS

Did you know that you can find patents for just about everything ever invented? You can... and you can use these patent filings any way you want.

For instance, you could create a book of all the patents that Thomas Edison filed or a book of the patents that most changed the world. Or if humor is more your style, a collection of funny patents could be a big success... Other topic ideas include "things you never knew existed", "famous patents of the 1890s", "women inventors and their patents" to name a few.

And since patents often have diagrams, the diagrams can often be the basis for neat coffee cups or t shirts.

# 47 CALENDARS

Calendars are pretty cool. Most people either buy or find a way to get one for free every year.

You can utilize the huge body of image work in the public domain to make your own themed calendars. The number of topics is virtually limitless...

How about early baseball players to sell to baseball themes, posters of World War II, Famous Architectural Models, early space flight, local historical images, etc. Whatever your imagination comes up with, you can probably find images to build the calendars.

The easiest way to sell such calendars is to find shows you can attend in the last four months of the year – civil war shows, community festivals, etc. But you could certainly build a website offering all your calendars and concentrate your efforts to building traffic to it during the off months and releasing your new annual calendars every year. It wouldn't be a difficult task to build up 50 to 100 or more different calendars to offer.

# 48 NOSTALGIA PRODUCTS

Nostalgia is big business. From people wanting things from the olden days to remind them of simpler times to restaurants seeking "artwork" to put on their walls to help create the mood they want, there are many avenues that can be pursued when marketing nostalgia.

Some things that could be considered nostalgia products include old newspapers, pictures of your town when you were a child, old images of favorite vacation spots, old movie posters and comic/pulp magazine covers. There are of course many others but this small list gives you an idea of what could be considered nostalgia. (Really, nostalgia items are items that give a person that warm fuzzy feeling in their belly as they trigger pleasant memories of the past so any product you can create that brings about that feeling is a nostalgia item.)

# 49 DATABASES

The government collects statistics on just about everything and all that information is available for your use.

Probably the best example of a government database that is used commercially in a big way is the census data that is collected every 10 years. There are huge companies that use this data to create a variety of very high priced products or use as the basis of expensive research reports they supply to their clients.

Another example of a government database is automobile recalls. It serves as a great supplement to a website about car safety issues.

There are literally hundreds of these databases that you can use. Many have no commercial interest but many do. You will need to do some research to find and determine which ones would be appropriate for your planned activities.

## 50 GENEALOGY

Ancestry research is big business. Just think of ancestry.com. They are always advertising on TV. And all the data that they offer their subscribers is public domain material.

Now, you do not need to be an ancestry.com to make good money in this business area. You can use your collating skills to make a variety of products related to ancestry – town records and histories, birth and death indexes, cemetery records, newspaper birth and obituary notices, family name histories, old phone books and business directories and on and on.

# 51 HISTORIC MAPS

There are tens of thousands of maps in the public domain. Some are plain looking maps like you would find in an atlas but many are works of art. And people collect these maps (or reproductions of them) for a variety of reasons.

It is a simple matter to find hundreds to thousands of very interesting maps that are already digitized and freely available for download on the web.

Combine those digital files with a website, a wide format printer and good quality paper and you are in business.

# 52 AFFILIATE LINKS

This is a pretty simple idea.

Take popular historical books, edit in affiliate links, convert them to PDF files and give them away for free.

If you pick the right types of books and get a decent amount of traffic to your website, you could soon be having thousands of downloads of your books every months... and some portion of the readers will click on your affiliate links and earn you commissions.

## 53 SEED A FORUM

Starting a forum is really difficult. No one wants to take the time to participate in a forum unless they see many other people participating. And lots of posts.

Public domain material can help you supercharge the launch of your forum. You literally have tons of information on almost any topics that you could copy pretty much as is to start hundreds of forum topics.

In fact, the hardest part of this seeding effort would be the time it takes to create a number of members so you can seed the topics (and responses to them) from a large number of people.

With a part time effort over a month or so, you can create the impression that there are hundreds of members and a very active forum.

## 54 TRANSLATION

If you have the ability to market in other languages, you could translate public domain works and expose them to an entirely new market.

There are lots of really great public domain works that have only been published in English. If you can translate them to Spanish, French, German, Italian, etc., you have an opportunity to sell lots of copies of these books to entire markets that have never been exposed to them.

## 55 CONTENT FOR REPLIES

A big part of building credibility – and traffic – on the web is your ability to provide good answers to question. In fact, there are entire services devoted to this. Yahoo answers is just one of them.

Public domain content will often supply you with high quality answers to questions asked on Yahoo answers, discussion forums and other places on the web.

So if you are familiar with your subject and the content of public domain resources in your subject area, you will be able to answer any questions that come up in just minutes by copying relevant public domain content and massaging it just a bit to exactly answer the specific question being asked.

# 56 INTERACTIVE WEBSITES

You can use public domain content to build a variety of interactive websites. These can be trivia websites, quiz websites, crossword puzzles, word finds, etc. There are free and low cost programming tools to help you create all these sorts of websites.

The idea is that you build a themed website, draw visitors to it and monetize the traffic.

# 57 BONUS PRODUCTS

Bonuses are big business. I can't quote any statistics because it would be different for different industries/offers but bonuses often help close the deal.

Are you selling a gardening product? Why not throw in a public domain product on tomato growing.

Are you offering a fly fishing product? How about several public domain books on fly fishing as the bonus.

You get the idea...

## 58 ENHANCE YOUR LIFE

Hey, not everything needs to be about money. So why not find some public domain works related to one of your hobbies and dive in. You just might find a few things that make your hobby that much more enjoyable.

# END NOTE

You have just been presented with 58 different ways you can use public domain works to improve your marketing, enhance your website content and generate new revenue streams. And this is just the beginning. For every place that you use content in any form, you can probably find public domain content that you can massage for that purpose.

Now it is time for you to take this knowledge and put it to use in your own business. Be adventurous and experiment with the ways you use this material. Only by doing this will you find the success formula that works best for you.

www.ingramcontent.com/pod-product-compliance
Lightning Source LLC
Chambersburg PA
CBHW021503210526
45463CB00002B/872